Sticks

The For Boys Only Version

By Penelope Dyan

Because Sticks Are Also People

Bellissima Publishing, LLC
Jamul, California
www.bellissimapublishing.com

copyright © 2008 by Penny D. Weigand

All rights reserved. No part of this book may be
reproduced or transmitted in any form or by any means,
electronic or mechanical, including photocopying,
recording, or by any other means, or by any information or
storage retrieval system, without permission from the publisher.

ISBN 1-935118-13-7
First Edition

For all the children who are sticks who happen to be boys

Sticks-The For Boys Only Version
Bellissima Publishing, LLC

Introduction

This is a great little book and this one is meant just for boys, the first book to be published in Penelope Dyan's "Penny Mouse Early Reader Series," in the For Boys Only Version. It is a book meant to encourage reading, creativity and the fun of learning all wrapped into one! The concept is simple, but the meaning is deep. Everything about Dyan is more than it seems and less than it seems. And basically, this is a book meant for fun that a teacher can either take into the classroom or a mom can read at home, and the beauty of the poetry line is that the children can guess what comes next and begin the process of reading as their minds gravitate toward the creative, To do a book like this, you have to be able think like a child. Dyan has certainly done that!

So parents, please enjoy this book with your kids, and teachers, please en joy yourselves as well, because this is exactly why Dyan created these books!

Watch for more Penny Mouse Early Readers,' because they will be coming out soon!

Written by a former teacher, and intended just for you, it's Penny Mouse all the way!

Sticks
Bellissima Publishing, LLC

Sticks

The For Boys Only Version

By Penelope Dyan

Because Sticks Are Also People

I am a stick person!

And Now I have hair!

I have eyes!

And feet!

And boys' underwear!

I have eyebrows and man eyelashes too!
This is something very new!

Now just look I found an ear,
And I have two so I can hear!

I discovered I have a hand!
I think that is very grand!

I discovered I have another!
It must have come right from my father!

I have something just like you,
I have a mouth and I can chew!

And lurking somewhere underneath,
I have a set of big white teeth!

And now it seems I must confess;
I am a boy! I'd never ever wear a dress!

If you think you have to stare,
Check out the hat that covers my hair!

Finally at last I have a nose;
Everyone needs one of those!

At my side I smell a pig!

There's another one, and it's kind of big!

I found some grass beneath my feet;
And I think that is really neat!

There are clouds in the sky and birds in the air;
From where they came I know not where!

Now I can really have some fun,
Because I see a great big sun!

Sticks-The For Boys Only Version
Bellissima Publishing, LLC

And here is something you can do,
Build a stick person just like you.
It is easy, as you just saw;
Pick up a pencil, some crayons, and start to draw!

Sticks-The For Boys Only Version
Bellissima Publishing, LLC